THE MARSHALL PLAN AND UNITED STATES POST WORLD WAR II INTERESTS IN EUROPE

CHAPTER I

INTRODUCTION AND BACKGROUND

General

December 7, 1941 is remembered as the day Japan "awakened a sleeping giant." However, America was never fully awakened until the latter years of the Second World War and the post-war period, when it finally began to accept its international responsibilities as the leader of the free world. During this time, American leaders and citizens alike began to understand the necessity for the U.S. to play a more active role in world affairs and abandon its longstanding policy of isolationism. They also realized that a healthy European and global economy was essential to U.S. prosperity, as was the promotion, growth and survival of free institutions. Thus the period 1944-1951 was one of the most important and decisive in U.S. and indeed world history.

The Marshall Plan played a key role in this historic era of American foreign policy by helping reconstruct and integrate Western Europe. It also bolstered the U.S. economy and created the framework for a political and military alliance that not only contained the spread of communism but has also produced over forty years of peace on that continent. Thus the Marshall Plan unquestionably played a central role in furthering U.S. post World War II interests in Europe. In fact, by integrating Western Europe economically, politically and militarily, this magnificent and enormously successful foreign policy initiative is still serving America's interests today.

Prelude to the Marshall Plan

It should be noted that while the Marshall Plan deserves much of the credit for reconstructing and integrating Western Europe as well as helping America fulfill its leadership role in world affairs, these processes had actually begun during the war. For example, in July 1944, the U.S. took the lead in making arrangements for the post-war world by hosting and orchestrating the celebrated 44 nation Breton Woods Conference in Breton Woods, New Hampshire. At this meeting (officially known as the United Nations Monetary and Financial Conference), the U.S. and other nations discussed post-war reconstruction needs and subsequently created the International Monetary Fund (IMF) and the International Bank for Reconstruction and Development (commonly known as the World Bank).

Like the Marshall Plan, these institutions not only helped make capital available to rebuild Europe but, ultimately, built the framework for free trade and lasting economic partnerships.

CHAPTER II

POST-WAR SETTING

The End of Isolationism

The painful experience of World War II against "two fanatical powers" made American leaders and citizens alike realize the price of isolationism.[1] Concomitantly, they also realized that their own security and prosperity could be and indeed were directly "affected by events beyond America's borders." [2] But, for several reasons, these realizations did not sink in quickly. First, U.S. "soil was untouched by the enemy."[3] Second, at the end of the war, the U.S. occupied a position of "unprecedented military and economic power·' and felt confident and secure about its future.[4] Third, the U.S. emerged from the war optimistic about the future of Europe and world affairs in general.

Together, these factors almost resulted in America returning to its longstanding practice of isolationism. However, the extent of the destruction in Europe, fears of a possible worldwide economic collapse, along with bold Soviet aggression and expansionism changed America's post-war expectations and prodded it to play a proactive and assertive role in international affairs. The Marshall Plan was one of the first and most significant indications of this shift in foreign policy. In fact, it played a key role in shaping the world as it is known today.

Conditions in Europe

At the end of World War II, the European economy was shattered. Its industrial base and cities were largely reduced to ashes and rubble.[5] Financial institutions were decimated and cash reserves were all but depleted. Unemployment was alarmingly high and there was a severe shortage of both food and housing. In other words, "the basic fabric of Europe's economy was falling apart."[6] These chaotic conditions caused tremendous anxiety not only in Europe but also in the United States which had been Europe's best trading partner before the war. Thus many Americans "feared the economic collapse of Europe would also result in the economic collapse of the U.S."[7] However, despite this anxiety and the widespread devastation, U.S. policymakers believed the recovery would be fairly rapid "because of the cooperation it expected from alliances that helped bring the war to a conclusion."[8] U.S. Expectations and Relations with the Soviets.

The seeds of optimism about Europe's future had been planted at Yalta and Potsdam, where Roosevelt and Truman believed "amicable relations had been established."[9] At Yalta, Roosevelt had high hopes of "big power cooperation" and thought it "laid the foundation for a stable world order."[10] Truman, like Roosevelt, hoped the Potsdam agreements "would help solve the economic and political problems of Europe in accordance with democratic principles."[11]

Stalin reinforced the allied good will at these historic meetings by "making concessions on a number of vital issues and promising good will for the future."[12] Thus President Truman's immediate post-war goals were to maintain the peace, restore Europe's economy, re-establish and revitalize U.S. economic ties, prevent territorial changes and expansion, and allow defeated enemy states to establish peaceful, democratic governments.[13] However, the "post-Yalta record showed it meant different things to its Anglo-American and Russian participants."[14] As Stalin had written in 1944, "the existence of the Soviet Republic side-by-side with imperialist states is unthinkable one or the other must triumph in the end."[15]

ENDNOTES

1 Michael J. Hogan, *The Marshall Plan: America, Britain and the Reconstruction of Western Europe 1947-1952*, Cambridge, Cambridge University Press, 1987, p. ix.

2. Albert H. Bowman and Orner de Raemaker, *American Foreign Policy in Europe,* New York, Humanities Press, 1969, p. 26.

3. Ernst Von der Beugel, *From Marshall Aid to Atlantic Partnership*, Amsterdam, Elsevier, 1966, p. 12.

4. William Reitzel, *United States Foreign Policy 1944-1955*, Washington, the Brookings Institution, 1956 p. 9.

5. Lewis P. Todd, ed., *The Marshall Plan: A Program of International Cooperation*, Washington, US Government Printing Office, 1978, p. 1.

6. Ibid.

7. Charles L. Mee, *The Marshall Plan: The Launching of Pax Americana*, New York, Simon and Schuster, 1984, p. 77.

8. Hogan, p. 29.

9. John Spanier, *American Foreign Policy Since World War II*, New York, Holt, Rinehart and Winston, 1983, p. 23.

10 Ibid.

11. Ibid., p. 24.

12. Ibid., p. 25.

13. Reitzel, p. 45.

14 James H. Johnson, *The Marshall Plan: A Case study in American Policy Formulation and Implementation*, Unpublished PHD Dissertation, Norman, OK, 1966, p. 9.

15. William H. Wilbur, *Guideposts to the Future: A New American Foreign Policy*, Chicago, Henry Regnery Company, 1954, p. 160.

CHAPTER III

SOVIET AGGRESSION AND EXPANSIONISM

Background

The first indications of the Soviet's true intentions came at the end of the war, when the Soviet Army continued its march on Eastern Europe. Another indication of its expansionist ambitions was the fact that it continued to have a large standing military after the war ended, while its wartime allies were demobilizing. Obviously, the soviets' actions were disturbing to the West, but the Soviet threat still did not strike home until the ill-fated Big Four (or Moscow) Conference in March 1947 on the future of Germany. Its failure to bring about an agreement and the antagonistic behavior of the Soviets convinced Secretary of State George c. Marshall that the soviets "were doing everything possible to exploit the already bleak situation in Europe."[1] In fact, Marshall concluded that the "Soviet Union was counting on the total collapse of Europe."[2]

This conclusion was particularly disturbing in view of Marshall's increasing concerns and personal observations that, despite $12 billion in aid ($9 billion from the U.S.) since the war, there were few tangible signs of economic recovery in Europe.[3] Indeed, Marshall now fully understood the cold reality of the situation and forthrightly acknowledged the need for U.S. and Europe to "act quickly to avert the impending collapse of all of Europe."[4]

Upon Marshall's return from Moscow, he reported his observations to President Truman and other American leaders who were equally concerned that the grim economic conditions in Europe had created a "political, social and psychological crisis" that provided fertile ground for the spread of communism.[5] These concerns were heightened by the "power vacuum created in Central and Western Europe by the defeat of Germany and the exhaustion of Britain and France."[6] This situation was exacerbated even more by growing communist parties in France and Italy. U.S. leaders finally recognized that they had "underestimated the effects of the war" and the full extent of Europe's economic disaster, political disorder and social unrest.[7] Furthermore, they now realized that

Western and Central Europe were the targets of Soviet subversion and aggression.

Early soviet Expansion

In reality, Soviet expansionism had already begun with the annexation of Estonia, Latvia and Lithuania-- together with parts of Finland, Rumania, Poland, Northeastern Germany and Eastern Czechoslovakia. These encroachments continued after the war as the Soviets consolidated their control over Eastern Europe.[8] "In less than a year, Moscow had succeeded in gaining control over the governments of Budapest, Sofia, Bucharest, Warsaw and Prague." They also "exerted heavy pressure directly or indirectly" in Northern Iran, Turkey, Greece, Indochina and Malaya.[9] Thus within two years after the war, "the communists controlled a large part of Europe, menaced the whole continent" and provoked unrest in other parts of the world.[10]

Crises in Greece and Turkey

The Soviets attempted to establish a foothold in Greece and Turkey by exploiting their loss of military and financial aid from Great Britain. In Greece, "a communist guerrilla movement threatened to topple the conservative government which had been elected after the war."[11] This guerrilla threat came from both inside and outside Greece's borders. However, "the most severe threat came from a team of communist guerrillas that kept pouring over Greece's northern border terrorizing towns, the countryside and threatening to build up to a full strength attack force."[12]

Turkey also became a target of Soviet expansionism after the Second World War, when the Soviets demanded certain Turkish territory be transferred to its control. Additionally, the Kremlin also tried to force Turkey to sign a treaty of cooperation and security similar to those it had with Eastern European nations.[13] Prior to 1947, British assistance enabled both Turkey and Greece to resist severe Soviet pressure. But without this help, "the situation was utterly precarious and their eventual collapse was inevitable."[14]

The situation in Greece and Turkey was of particular concern, because their "loss would have a profound impact on other European nations struggling to survive and recover from the war."[15] The U.S. was also concerned about the potential loss of these nations because "they controlled the access to sea trade to the Middle East and were close to important oil resources on which Anglo-American interests depended."[16] President Truman wanted "to retain access to these vital resources and keep them out of the Soviet sphere of influence."[17] Hence "the specter of growing communism did not simply outrage American humanitarianism but, more importantly, it seriously threatened U.S. national interests in the largest sense."[18] Consequently, it became apparent that "the crises in Greece and Turkey were indications of a much wider, impending catastrophe that also had dire implications for all of Europe and for the U.S."[19] Therefore, Truman and other American leaders realized America's security and prosperity were directly affected by events in Greece and Turkey, and spread of communism, and the possible denial of access to world markets.

ENDNOTES

1. Harry B. Price, *The Marshall Plan and Its Meaning,* Ithaca, Cornell University Press, 1955, p. 4.

2. Hans A. Schmitt, *The Path to European Union: From the Marshall Plan to the Common Market,* Baton Rouge, Louisiana State University Press, 1962, p. 20.

3. James H. Johnson, *The Marshall Plan: A Case study in American Policy Formulation and Implementation*, Unpublished PHD Dissertation, Norman, OK, 1966, p. 49.

4. Price, pp. 143 and 144.

5. Charles L. Mee, Jr., *The Marshall Plan: The Launching of Pax Americana,* New York, Simon and Schuster, 1984, p. 89.

6. Michael J. Hogan, *The Marshall Plan: America, Britain, and the Reconstruction of Western Europe 1947-1952*, Cambridge, Cambridge University Press, 1987, p. 27.

7. Ernst Hans von der Beugel, *From Marshall Aid to Atlantic Partnership,* Amsterdam, Elsevier, 1966, p. 35.

8. The *North Atlantic Treaty Organization: Facts and Figures*, NATO Information Service, Brussels, 1984, p. 14.

9. Ibid., p. 16

10. Sir Nicholas Henderson, *The Birth of NATO, Boulder, Westview Press,* 1983, p. xiii.

11. "The Marshall Plan: *Origins and Implementation." Bureau of Public Affairs Bulletin,* Washington, us Government Printing Office, 1987, p. 2.

12. Charles A. Cerami, *Alliance Born of Danger: The Common Market & The Atlantic Partnership*, New York, Harcourt, Brace & World Inc., 1963, p. 17.

13. Ernst Hans von der Beugel, *From Marshall Aid to Atlantic Partnership*, Amsterdam, Elsevier, 1966, p. 23.

14. Ibid.

15. Lawrence s. Kaplan, *NATO & The Policy of Containment*, Boston, Heath and Company, 1968, pp. 5 and 6.

16. Barton J. Bernstein, ed., *Politics and Policies of the Truman Administration,* Chicago, QuadrangleBooks,1970, p. 12.

17. Ibid.

18. Ibid., p. 57.

19. Johnson, p. 323

CHAPTER IV

U.S. REACTION AND RESPONSE

Reassessment of Soviet and U.S. Foreign Policy

The situation in Greece and Turkey caused American leaders to "reassess Soviet foreign policy as well as their own."[1] They realized that "peace, freedom and world trade were inseparable." [2] Additionally, they recognized that economic stability went hand-in-hand with political stability. This fact was especially worrisome since "the political situation in Europe was a mirror image of the grim economic conditions."[3] There was no question that U.S. prosperity was inextricably tied to Europe's economy. President Truman and others realized that "without economic assistance Europe would be unable to defend itself and thus would be lost and World War III would be inevitable."[4] He also realized that an economically vibrant Western Europe would not only help stop the spread of communism but could also pay large, long-term dividends to the U.S. economy. Additionally, access to European markets and raw materials were necessary for the development of atomic energy.

[5]Therefore, America's new strategy would necessarily have to focus on the economic reconstruction of Europe in a manner that produced not only economic recovery and integration but political and military partnerships as well.

Aid to Greece and Turkey

W. Averell Harriman, Ambassador to the Soviet Union, was one of the first administration officials to propose America attempt to solve its problems with the Soviets by using its economic power. He suggested the U.S. use its economic resources to "assist those countries that were naturally friendly to our concepts."[6] Harriman's position was a "realization that U.S. security had become directly dependent on the creation and maintenance of partnerships that insured its economic wellbeing as well as resisted communist expansionism."[7]

President Truman agreed with his Soviet Ambassador and others who advocated this approach.   Thus he embarked his administration on an effort to develop a strategy and policy that would ameliorate the catastrophes in Greece and Turkey and expedite the recovery of Europe. Therefore, U.S. objectives in Europe were to restore Europe, re-establish economic ties, contain Soviet expansionism, and create a defensive security alliance.

Containment Policy

George F. Kennan, a State Department Soviet expert, was the acknowledged architect of containment policy, in which the Marshall Plan would play a crucial role. In his famous "Sources of Soviet Conduct" article, Kennan highlighted Soviet expansionist tendencies as well as the irreconcilable differences between capitalism and socialism.[8] He then prescribed a policy of containment to enable America to "confront the Russians...at every point where they showed signs of encroaching upon the interests of a peaceful and stable world."[9] His policy of containment quickly became the cornerstone of the Truman Doctrine and began a new era in U.S. foreign policy, requiring America to play a more active role in international affairs and end its long history of isolationism.

Kennan's containment policy and the Truman Doctrine had three primary objectives:

> (a) to restore the international balance of power, thereby preventing the Soviet Union from exploiting power vacuums left by the defeats of Germany and Japan; (b) to reduce the Soviet Union's ability to project influence beyond its borders through the international communist movement; and (c) to ultimately bring about, through a combination of

inducements and deterrents, a modification in the behavior of the Soviet leadership toward the outside world which would cause it to learn to live with, rather than seek to eliminate, diversity.[10][10]

Truman Doctrine

President Truman first proclaimed his doctrine and the policy of containment in March 1947, when he requested military and economic aid to help Greece and Turkey defeat communist encroachments. In an emotional speech before Congress, Truman stated that a number of countries had totalitarian regimes forced upon them and that "such action undermined international peace and hence the security of the United States." He declared that "it must be the policy of the United States to support free peoples who are resisting subjugation by armed minorities or by outside pressures." Truman also pointed out that "the consequences of failing to provide aid would be far reaching to the West and to the East." He concluded by saying that U.S. assistance "should be primarily through economic and financial aid which is essential to economic stability and orderly political processes." [11]

President Truman's request for aid received overwhelming bipartisan support from Congress, which shared his fears and mistrust of the soviets. Thus American began what Kennan described as a "long-term patient but firm policy of containment."[12]

ENDNOTES

(1.) John Spanier, *American Foreign Policy Since World War II*, New York, Holt, Rinehart and Winston, 1983, p. 47.

(2.) Barton J. Bernstein, ed., Politics and Policies of the Truman Administration, Chicago, Quadrangle Books, 1970, p. 78.

(3.) Ibid., p. 81.

(4.) Ibid., p 80.

(5.) Ibid., p. 91.

(6.) Ibid., p. 26.

(7.) Arnold Wolfers, *Alliance Policy in the Cold War*, Baltimore, Johns Hopkins Press, 1958. P. 16.

(8.) George F. Kennan, *"Sources of Soviet Conduct,"* Foreign Affairs, July 1947, p. 853.

(9.) Ibid.

(10.) John L. Gaddis, *Strategies of containment: A Critical Appraisal of Postwar American National Security Foreign Policy*, New York, Oxford University Press, 1982, pp. 36 and 37.

(11.) Thomas G. Patterson, *Containment and the Cold War: American Foreign Policy Since 1945*, Reading, Addison Wesley Publishing Company. 1973, pp. 15 and 16.

(12.) Kennan, p. 854.

<u>Marshall's Proposal</u>

Shortly after Congress approved aid for Greece and Turkey, Secretary Marshall made his famous speech at Harvard University in June 1947 in which he proposed a much larger comprehensive program be undertaken to restore Europe's economy. In his speech, Marshall described the bleak situation in Europe and its potential long-term consequences for America. Thus his proposal "rested squarely on the American conviction that Europe's economic recovery was essential to U.S. security and prosperity."[1]
Marshall's plan called for a program of massive aid to revive Europe's economy and create conditions "in which free institutions can exist."[2] He emphasized that "substantial help" would be needed and that "the initiative" for such a program had to "come from within Europe." [3] In other words, it could only succeed with Europe's full participation.

"The Marshall Plan was more than just a reaction to a particular crisis. It reflected more than just a desire to alleviate distress. It was a recognition that these goals could no longer be pursued in isolation."[4] Thus the Marshall Plan had a "much broader objective...based on the proposition that its success would require close cooperation among aid recipients and, more importantly, that Western Europe's economic as well as political strength would ultimately lead to European unity and a coalition security alliance."[5]

An Invitation Open to All Nations

The U.S. was careful to invite **all** nations to participate in the Marshall Plan and not to direct it against any nation. Dean Acheson and George Kennan advised this approach for several reasons. First, they did not want Marshall's plan to be identified as a deliberate attempt to divide Europe. Second, they did not think the Soviet Union would participate in such a program, because of its likely unwillingness to relinquish control of its economy and expose its widespread internal problems. Third, in the event that the Soviets chose to participate, they could make a genuine contribution. Lastly, a Soviet rejection would galvanize support for the plan, because it would be perceived that the communists were opposed to a European recovery.[6]

Soon after Marshall's speech, a conference of European nations was held in Paris to discuss his proposal. soviet Foreign Minister Molotov rejected the Marshall Plan on several grounds. First, he claimed it "constituted an interference in the internal affairs of European nations" and would thus violate their national sovereignty. Second, Molotov accused France and Great Britain of "scheming to use the Marshall Plan to increase their influence in the region and assure a predominant position in the proposed organization." Third, he attacked the proposal as a "selfish, imperialistic endeavor that would give the U.S. a decisive hold on Europe." Finally, Molotov said the plan was "another attempt to pressure, isolate and challenge communist nations."[7]

"In a practical sense, the Soviets could not have accepted membership in an organization dominated and directed by Americans and motivated by a desire to curb Soviet influence in the world."[8] This was reinforced by the fact that Marshall's speech had "followed closely behind...many anti-Soviet speeches by (American) government officials."[9] Thus the U.S. correctly anticipated the soviets' rejection and saw the Marshall Plan as a means not only to help Europe recover but also to "break Soviet influence in Eastern Europe."[10]

<u>Soviet Response</u>

Stalin responded to Marshall's initiative by forming the Communist Information Bureau (Cominform) in September 1947, whose aim was to "fight the Marshall Plan as an instrument of American imperialism."[11] Its members included the communist parties of the Soviet Union,

Yugoslavia, Hungary, Poland, Bulgaria, Czechoslovakia, Rumania and, curiously, the Netherlands and France (which later withdrew). The purpose of this organization was to coordinate communist movements in various countries such as Greece and Turkey.[12] Thus what Acheson, Kennan and other American policymakers had anticipated was now a reality--Europe was divided into two camps.

Interim Aid

About the same time the Cominform was established, it became obvious to the U.S. that "France, Italy and Austria would not be able to survive the winter of 1947-48 without widespread suffering unless they received help."[13] Congress responded by authorizing over $500 million in assistance.[14] Soviet attempts to disrupt the Marshall Plan only hastened its acceptance. The interim U.S. aid and attempts to ameliorate deteriorating conditions throughout Europe "mobilized support" for the plan and "generated a sense of urgency on both sides of the Atlantic that expedited its approval and implementation."[15]

Berlin Blockade

The Soviet blockade of Berlin in June 1948 is a dramatic illustration of how their attempts to disrupt the Marshall Plan "backfired." Both Western Europe and the U.S. moved quickly to rectify this situation and ultimately used it against the Soviets. It was then that American "sensed the greater implications" of Marshall's brilliant plan.[16]

ENDNOTES

1. Michael J. Hogan, *The Marshall Plan: America, Britain, and the Reconstruction of Western Europe 1947-1952*, Cambridge, Cambridge University Press, 1987, p. 26.

2. *The Marshall Plan and the Future of US European Relations*, New York, German Information Center, 1953, pp. 8 and 9.

3. Ibid.

4. Harry B. Price, *The Marshall Plan and Its Meaning*, Ithaca, Cornell University Press, 1955, p. 6.

5. Immanuel Wexler, *The Marshall Plan Revisited: The European Recovery Program in Economic Perspective,* Westport, Greenwood Press, 1983, p. 205.

6. Hans A. Schmitt, *The Path to European Union: From the Marshall Plan to the Common Market,* Baton Rouge, Louisiana State University Press, 1962, pp. 21 and 22.

7. James H. Johnson, *The Marshall Plan: A Case Study in American Policy Formulation and Implementation*, Unpublished PHD Dissertation, Norman OK, 1966, pp. 160 and 161.

8. Barton J. Bernstein, ed., *Politics and Policies of the Truman Administration,* Chicago, Quadrangle Books, 1970, p. 101.

9. Ibid.

10. Hogan, p. 52

11. *The North Atlantic Treaty Organization: Facts and Figures*, Brussels, NATO Information Service, 1984, p. 19.

12. Ibid.

13. Hogan, p. 84.

14. Ibid.

15. Ibid, p. 56.

16. Price, p. 5.

Goals

In April 1948, Congress passed the Marshall Plan or European Cooperation Act and created the European Recovery Program (ERP), the official name for the Marshall Plan. In this four year program, Congress "mandated a recovery effort based on four economic endeavors: (1) a strong production effort, (2) the expansion of foreign trade, (3) the creation and maintenance of internal financial stability, and (4) the development of European economic cooperation."[1] The ERP provided $5.3 billion in initial aid and established the Economic Cooperation Administration (ECA) to oversee the program.[2]

Europe's Reaction

Europe reacted "quickly and enthusiastically." Its support for the plan was based on "the real hope and promise this program offered to relieve Europe of its economic disaster, political disorder and social unrest."[3]

It should be noted that the U.S. decided to organize the recovery effort outside of the United Nation's Economic Commission for Europe. This was because the U.S. felt it was "inappropriate for the UN to manage a U.S. sponsored program because of Soviet Union and Eastern European representation on the commission."[4] It should also be noted that many Western European nations were anxious and apprehensive about Germany's participation in the Marshall Plan. This was because of their fears that a resurrected Germany would possibly result in a rearmed and hence a hostile or threatening Germany. The U.S. allayed these fears by restricting Germany's initial role in the recovery program.

Economic Cooperation Administration

The ECA was headed by Mr. Paul G. Hoffman, a business executive, who was charged with administering the massive recovery program. However, as Marshall implied in his speech at Harvard, the keys to such a program were self-help, cooperation and mutual assistance. Therefore, the ECA administered aid through the Organization for European Economic Cooperation (OEEC), which consisted of 16 nations (Austria, Belgium, Denmark, France, Great Britain, Greece, Iceland, Ireland, Italy, Luxembourg, the Netherlands, Norway, Portugal, sweden, Switzerland and Turkey).

The purpose of the OEEC was to promote economic growth and increase trade among its members. It was also responsible for presenting requests for aid to the ECA for approval and then overseeing their distribution to OEEC members. Therefore, while the U.S. financed a large part of the ERP, it was administered by Western European nations. Thus the key letter in the titles of the ECA and the OEEC was "C"--which stood for cooperation. For indeed cooperation proved to be the keystone to the successful reconstruction of Europe. This also took on greater importance as the U.S. and OEEC members began to realize the importance of an economically and politically unified Western Europe.

ERP Aid

The bulk of ERP aid was used to finance essential imports and modernize facilities. It helped restore and construct steel mills, railroads, hydro-electric plants, agriculture and machinery factories, and much needed housing. An important aspect of the ERP was the use of counterpart funds. These were funds recipient governments invested that were equivalent to amounts received in U.S. grants. They were used to increase domestic production and were instrumental in expediting Europe's recovery. [5]

Early ERP Results

The first tangible results of economic recovery (e.g., high production, lower unemployment, etc.) began to appear across Western Europe in the latter part of 1948 and early 1949. However, the ERP's success became even more apparent in late 1949 when agricultural and industrial production increased to their pre-war levels.[6] This was indeed significant progress. However, equally significant was the fact that, by this time, the governments of France and Italy had all but eliminated communists from their cabinets.[7] This was compelling evidence that the Marshall Plan was fulfilling its implied political mission of helping stop the spread of communism.

Technical and Production Assistance Programs

By 1950, the ERP generated momentum and progress in almost every measurable economic area. This was a result of not only monetary aid but also technical assistance that improved productivity.

The Technical Assistance and Productivity Assistance Programs were key parts of the recovery program. They provided for the transfer of skill, knowledge and technology to plant owners, managers and union leaders. Thus while these programs were the least costly aspects of the ERP, they were perhaps the most important. They not only provided information vital to the recovery effort, but they also reinforced the "attitudes, habits and values ••of capitalism and democracy" that made Europe economically successful before the war.[8] Hence without doubt, they contributed substantially to Europe's restoration and helped forge a Western European and American partnership.

ENDNOTES

(1) Immanuel Wexler, *The Marshall Plan Revisited: The European Recovery Program in Economic Perspective,* Westport, Greenwood Press, 1983, p. 250.

(2) Ibid.

(3) Hadley Arkes, *Bureaucracy, the Marshall Plan and the National Interest,* Princeton, Princeton University Press, 1972, p. 201.

(4) Michael J. Hogan, *The Marshall Plan: America. Britain, and the Reconstruction of Western Europe 1947-1952,* Cambridge, Cambridge University Press, 1987, pp. 52 and 53.

(5) Harry B. Price, *The Marshall Plan and Its Meaning,* Ithaca, Cornell University Press, 1955, p. 67.

(6) Arkes, p. 76.

(7) Ibid.

(8) Hogan, p. 415.

CHAPTER VII MARSHALL PLAN RESULTS

Economic Results

By 1951, support for the Marshall Plan began to decline as both Europe and America shifted their attention to events in Korea and began focusing more on security matters. When it officially ended in December 1951, the ERP had distributed over $12 billion in aid, mostly in the form of grants to OEEC members. "This amount represented approximately 1.2 percent of the total U.S. gross national product (GNP) for calendar yearsx1948-1951[1]. Contrary to popular opinion, through counterpart fund program, Europe bore the brunt of the financial burden by providing seventy-five percent of the aid, the other twenty-five percent coming from the U.S.).

As shown below, U.S. ERP support declined in each of the four years of its existence.[3]

$ Billions	Year
4.97	1948
3.78	1949
2.31	1950
1.02	1951

During its almost four year formal existence, the Marshall Plan achieved remarkable success. Steel production doubled and overall industrial output increased forty percent above pre-war levels. Agricultural production also rose twenty percent.[4]

All of this served to "fuel economic growth and significantly raise living standards."[5] OEEC members realized a 33.5 percent increase in their per capita GNP and "a substantial renewal of their industrial base."[6] Further, the ERP helped create a network of strong economic ties between OEEC members and the U.S. This yielded long-term benefits for all concerned. For example, between 1948 and 1951, intra- European trade expanded by over seventy percent. Likewise, European exports and imports increased by sixty-six and twenty percent, respectively.[7]

Political Results

The political results of the Marshall Plan were equally impressive. While all was not a bed of roses among OEEC members during the ERP, occasional political bickering and incidents of selfishness were completely overshadowed by the unprecedented degree of cooperation among sovereign states. The Marshall Plan, therefore, helped to produce remarkable political stability and alleviate the social unrest and deprivation Truman said were the breeding ground for communism. Thus "the real value of the plan was its psychological and political by-products."[8] By resurrecting a shattered economy, the Marshall Plan also enhanced democratic principles and movements in Europe, thereby reducing opportunities for Soviet exploitation and expansionism. It also "created a sense of indebtedness and a reservoir of good will among Europeans toward America" that provided the foundation for the development of a strong political and military alliance system.

ENDNOTES

1. Immanuel Wexler, T*he Marshall_Plan Revisited: The European Recovery Program in Economic Perspective*, Westport, Greenwood Press, 1983, p. 249.

2. Lewis P. Todd, ed., *The Marshall Plan: A Program of International Cooperation*, Washington, US Government Printing Office, 1978, p. 7.

3. Harry B. Price, *The Marshall Plan and Its Meaning, Ithaca*, Cornell University Press, 1955, p. 88.

4. Michael J. Hogan, The Marshall Plan: America, Britain and the Reconstruction of Western Europe 1947-1952, Cambridge, Cambridge University Press, 1987, p. 431.

5. "The Marshall Plan: Origins and Implementation," *Bureau of Public Affairs Bulletin,* Washington, us Government Printing Office, April 1947, p. 14.

6. Ibid.

7. Wexler, p. 252.

8. Charles L. Mee, The Marshall Plan: The Launching of Pax Americana, New York, Simon and Schuster, 1984, p. 90.

9. "*The Marshall Plan: Origins and Implementation*," pp. 14 and 15.

CHAPTER VIII

END OF RECOVERY AND BEGINNING OF AN ALLIANCE

Invasion of Korea

"Prior to 1950, American leaders relied more on economic rather than military instruments to achieve their goals in Western Europe." In other words, "recovery had priority over rearmament."However, "by the spring of 1950, revived production and new signs of financial stability generated greater emphasis on rearmament which now had parity with recovery."[1] The communist invasion of South Korea in June of 1950 thus brought security measures to "center stage" and "shocked both U.S. and Western leaders into rearmament."[2]

This change did not occur suddenly, for in 1949 the European Cooperation Act was amended to add language encouraging the unification of Europe--thereby signaling the significance the U.S. placed on an economically, politically and militarily united Europe.[3] Earlier, the Soviet blockade of Berlin had influenced the U.S. to pursue security initiatives conceived during the crises in Greece and Turkey. Furthermore, "as the ERP began to produce results, and the need for raw materials grew, the relationship between industrial needs and security needs became clearer."[4]

Transformation from Economic Recovery to Mutual Security

The outbreak of the Korean conflict alarmed Western Euro e and America and convinced them that the same principles of <u>cooperation</u> and <u>unity</u> that characterized the ERP would be necessary to organize a successful security alliance. Thus the Marshall Plan was instrumental in the formation of such as effort.

Dunkirk and Brussels Treaties

Other events that contributed to the transition from an economic partnership to a security alliance included the Dunkirk and Brussels Treaties of 1947 and 1948. These were the forebearers of the North Atlantic Treaty and helped pave the way for a defensive alliance system.[5]

At a September 1948 meeting of the Western Union Defense Organization, the Canadian delegation recommended the establishment of a single mutual defensive alliance system, including and superseding those established by the Brussels and Dunkirk Treaties.[7] The U.S. responded by passing a widely supported resolution authored by Senator Vandenberg that authorized the U.S. "to develop collective arrangements within the charter of the United Nations."[8]

North Atlantic Treaty

The result of the Canadian suggestion and the Vandenberg Resolution was the North Atlantic Treaty which was ratified in June 1949. This treaty established the North Atlantic Treaty Organization (NATO), whose membership closely resembled the OEEC's. Thus NATO was a "logical consequence" or follow-on to the Marshall Plan, because it was organized along the same framework and emphasized both self-help and mutual cooperation.[9] For example, "Article 3 of the treaty stated that the parties separately and jointly, by means of continuous and effective **self-help** and **mutual aid** will maintain and develop their individual and collective capacity to resist armed attack."[10] In other words, the "ERP model" of cooperation and unity "was applied to the military sphere ..so as not to sacrifice economic and political gains made during the recovery."[11]

Mutual Defense Assistance Act

The Mutual Defense Assistance Act of September 1949 closely followed the North Atlantic Treaty. This act authorized the U.S. to provide arms and equipment to NATO countries.[12] In July 1950, it was amended to expand existing military programs.[13]

Mutual Security Program

"By the summer of 1951, military security had superseded self-reliance as the primary objective of American policy in Western Europe. This transition to security concerns was formalized by the termination of the ECA at the end of 1951 and the launching of the Mutual Security Program.

The conflict in Korea and increased Cold War tensions, particularly in Europe, were the primary factors for this transition. However, another factor was the considerable progress made in Europe's recovery as a result of the Marshall Plan. This enabled Western European nations and America to devote more resources to security initiatives.[15] As a result, "NATO countries increased defense spending from $4.2 billion to $8 billion in 1951."[16]

The October 1951 Mutual Security Act "abolished the Economic Cooperation Administration and in its place established the Mutual Security Agency (MSA)."[17] Its first director was W. Averell Harriman, who supervised all foreign aid programs (military, economic and technical).[18] However, the bulk of Harriman's duties were oriented toward defense or security programs. Thus with the creation of NATO and the MSA, the Marshall Plan was transformed into a security coalition.

ENDNOTES

1. Michael J. Hogan, <u>The Marshall Plan</u>: America, Britain and the Reconstruction of Western Europe 1947-1952, Cambridge, Cambridge University Press, 1987, p. 311.

2. Harry B. Price, <u>The Marshall Plan and Its Meaning,</u> Ithaca, Cornell University Press, 1955, p. 133.

3. William Reitzel, <u>United States Foreign Policy 1944-1955,</u> Washington, the Brookings Institution, 1956, pp. 121 and 122.

4. Ibid., p. 136.

5. Price, p. 281.

6. <u>The North Atlantic Treaty Organization: Facts and Figures,</u> Brussels, NATO Information Service, 1984, p. 19.

7. <u>Ibid.,</u> p 20.

8. Lewis P. Todd, ed., <u>The Marshall Plan: A Program of International Cooperation,</u> Washington, US Government Printing Office, 1978, p. 44.

9. Albert H. Bowman and Orner de Raemaker, American <u>Foreign Policy in Europe,</u> New York, Humanities Press, 1969, page 9.

10. Todd, pp.44-45.

11. Hogan, p. 312

12. Todd

13. Price, p. 136

14. Ibid., p. 161

15. Hogan, p. 337

16. Ibid., p. 393

17. Price, p. 165

18. Ibid

CHAPTER IX
CRITICISMS

General

Despite the Marshall Plan's immense success, it was nevertheless criticized on three major grounds. First, its critics argue that it divided Europe economically, politically and militarily[1] The second criticism, closely related to the first, was that the Marshall Plan and Truman Doctrine significantly increased Cold War tensions. Third, critics argue that, since America had the most to gain from Europe's recovery, its primary motivation was greed, not generosity.

Distinctions Between the Marshall Plan and Truman Doctrine

When historians discuss, praise or criticize the Marshall Plan, they generally consider it to be closely associated, if not synonymous with, the Truman Doctrine and containment policy. Walter Lippman, however, drew a sharp distinction between them. He considered the Marshall Plan a policy that "treated European governments as independent powers." Conversely, he thought containment policy "treated those who were supposed to benefit by it as dependencies of the United States."[2] Therefore, Mr. Lippman concluded that containment policy and Truman Doctrine were "unworkable in Europe" and that is why the Marshall Plan was developed (i.e., to offset the dependency problems inherent in containment policy).[3] However, while it is true that the Truman Doctrine and the Marshall Plan were undoubtedly distinguishable, it is also true that they were closely intertwined policies that had the same objectives--the reconstruction of Europe, the containment of communism, and the creation of economic, political and military partnerships. foreign policy. Therefore, they were integral parts of the same foreign policy.[4]

Another criticism aimed at the Marshall Plan over the years was that it was too expensive to the American taxpayer. However, this argument never carried much weight, since it is widely accepted that in the long run Americans benefitted substantially from the markets the Marshall Plan helped create. Furthermore, the ERP was "cheaper than the economic and political posts that would have resulted from a massive rearmament program the U.S. would have surely embarked on if the Soviets gained control of Western Europe."[5]

The economic, political, socio-psychological and military results of the Marshall Plan indicate that its criticisms are not without some foundation. Undoubtedly, it was a "political plan couched in economic terms and a mixture of generosity and self-interest."[6] However, it seems clear that the Marshall Plan's remarkable results and residual political and military benefits significantly outnumbered its shortcomings and expense.[7] In fact, the real key to the Marshall Plan's success was its skillful integration of the other elements of national power.

Burdensharing

Even the most ardent critics of the Marshall Plan and the North Atlantic Treaty generally agree on the phenomenal success of these historic foreign policy initiatives. Since their inception, however, they have raised the divisive issue of burdensharing--and continue to do so. Essentially, this boils down to the fact that the U.S. assumed a disproportionate share of the cost for both the recovery and the defense of Western Europe.

Today, the burdensharing debate has taken on a new spark and there are rekindled calls for other NATO nations to bear a greater share of the burden for their own security. There are several reasons for the burdensharing debate's new intensity. First, the Soviets do not appear quite as menacing or threatening as they have in the past due to Gorbachev's bold reform proposals, peace initiatives, and overall image as a diplomat and not a warrior. This apparently diminished Soviet challenge, coupled with the perception that "peace is breaking out all over," has reinvigorated the belief that the U.S. can and should reduce its commitments to NATO without degrading the security of Western Europe.

Another reason the issue of burdensharing is on the minds of many Americans is the status of America's economic health. Thus it is understandable that, in view of the staggering U.S. budget deficit, large trade imbalances and increasing commitments abroad, there are calls for America to reassess its foreign policy.

The third major reason why burdensharing is a "hot topic" is that Western Europe is in an economic position to assume a more equal share of the cost for its defense. This fact, coupled with Gorbachev's "glasnost" and "perestroika," will continue to pressure both the U.S. and NATO to address the delicate but profoundly important issue of burdensharing.

ENDNOTES

1. Charles L. Mee Jr., *The Marshall Plan: The Launching of Pax Americana,* New York, Simon and Schuster, 1984, pp. 205 and 206.

2. Walter J. Lippman, The Cold War," *New York Herald Tribune,* 1947, Reprinted Foreign Affairs, Spring 1987, p. 110.

3. Ibid., p. 111.

4. Ernst Hans von der Beugel, *From Marshall Aid to Atlantic Partnership,* Amsterdam, Elsevier, 1966, p. 28.

5. Michael J. Hogan, The Marshall Plan: America, *Britain and the Reconstruction of Western Europe 1947-1952,* Cambridge, Cambridge University Press, 1987, p. 190.

6. Immanuel Wexler, *The Marshall Plan Revisited: The European Recovery in Economic Perspective,* Westport, Greenwood Press, 1983, p. 250.

7. Hogan, p. 190.

CHAPTER X CONCLUSION

Unquestionably, the Marshall Plan played a pivotal and central role in helping the U.S. achieve its post-World War II objectives in Europe. It did so by rehabilitating Western Europe's economy and producing the political stability necessary to both resist and contain communist subversion and aggression. Thus it is clear that the designers of the Marshall Plan understood not only its short-term economic significance but, more importantly, its long-term political and military implications as well.

The Marshall Plan was a "key element" in America's goal for a stabilized Europe and "launched the U.S. into an era of unprecedented partnership and cooperation with its (Western Europe) allies."[1] It also "led to the creation of institutions such as the Common Market, European Economic Council and organization for Economic Development that are the pillars of the free world's economy."[2]

Marshall's European Recovery Program also laid the groundwork for the North Atlantic Treaty Organization--a collective security mechanism that has furthered U.S. interests through a coalition of forward deployed forces. This alliance is one of the "longest and most successful in history."[3]

The Marshall Plan began as an economic initiative but evolved into a larger more comprehensive program. "It combined reconstruction with the building of an economic, political and military alliance."[4] Thus it "demonstrated the linkage between prosperity and political stability" and is a superb "example of enlightened diplomacy."[5]

In conclusion, the Marshall Plan was a phenomenal foreign policy success that was brilliant in its design, sophisticated in its execution and far-reaching in its effects. America's interests were indeed well served by the Marshall Plan and the forty years of peace, prosperity and political stability it helped bring about in Europe.

ENDNOTES

1. Ronald Reagan, "The Legacy of the Marshall Plan, *Bureau of Public Affairs Bulletin,* Washington, us Government Printing Office, June 1987, p. 1.

2. Ibid p. 2

3. Arthur Cyr, *U.S. Foreign Policy & European Security*, New York, St. Martin's Press, 1987, p. 10.

4. Lawrence s. Kaplan, NATO & The United States: The Enduring Alliance, Boston, Twayne Publishers, 1988, p. 27.

5. George Shultz, "The 40th Anniversary of the Marshall Plan," *Bureau of Public Affairs Bulletin,* Washington, US Government Printing Office, June 1987, p. 2.

www.ingramcontent.com/pod-product-compliance
Lightning Source LLC
Chambersburg PA
CBHW052029280526

45793CB00005B/1174